A COMPREHENSIVE TO COMPUTER BASICS

LEARNERS GUIDE

NAVEEN SHARMA

Made with ♥ on the Notion Press Platform
www.notionpress.com

Contents

Preface

The use of computers has revolutionized the way we work, communicate, and live our lives. Computers offer a range of benefits, from increased productivity and enhanced communication to improved data management and efficient task automation. With the help of computers, businesses can easily store, access, analyze, and share data in real time. Additionally, businesses can use computers to automate repetitive tasks which helps reduce labor costs and increase efficiency. Computers also facilitate communication across businesses and organizations by enabling online meetings, video conferencing, and other forms of electronic communication. Furthermore, computers provide entertainment and education opportunities through the internet and various types of software. Finally, the use of computers has greatly enhanced the way people interact by connecting them with friends, family, and colleagues from around the world.

CHAPTER I

Introduction

Computers have become an essential part of our lives, and with that comes a lot of responsibility. While computers are easy to use, there are a few basics that everyone should know in order to stay safe and protect their data. In this post, we are going to provide you with a comprehensive guide to computer basics. From understanding the different parts of a computer to protecting your data, we will cover everything you need to know in order to use computers safely and protect your information. By the end of this post, you will have everything you need to start using computers safely and understand the basics of computer security. So whether you are a beginner or a more experienced user, make sure to read through this guide to get started.

CHAPTER II

Overview of Microsoft Word

Microsoft Word is a popular word processing software used to create and edit documents. Here is a complete guide to using Microsoft Word:

1. Getting Started with Microsoft Word:

- Launch Microsoft Word on your computer.
- You will be greeted with the Start Screen, which offers various options to create a new document or open an existing one.
- Select the option that suits your needs.

1. Creating a New Document:

- To create a new document, select the "Blank document" option from the Start Screen or click on "New" from the File menu.
- Once you have created a new document, you can begin typing in your text.

3. Formatting Text:

- To format text, select the text you want to format and use the various options in the Home tab to change the font, size, color, and other text attributes.
- You can also use the Styles gallery to quickly apply pre-defined styles to your text.

4. Inserting Objects:

- You can insert various objects into your document, such as pictures, tables, charts, and shapes.

- To insert an object, select the Insert tab and choose the appropriate option.

5. Editing and Proofreading:

- You can edit your document using the various editing tools in Word, such as copy, paste, cut, find and replace, and more.
- You can also use the Spelling and Grammar check to proofread your document.

6. Saving and Sharing:

- To save your document, click on the File menu and select "Save" or "Save As".
- You can also share your document with others by using the "Share" option in the File menu.

7. Printing:

- To print your document, click on the File menu and select "Print".
- You can also use the Print Preview option to preview your document before printing.

8. Advanced Features:

- Microsoft Word has many advanced features, such as creating a Table of Contents, adding footnotes and endnotes, creating macros, and more.
- You can explore these features by using the Help menu or by taking a Microsoft Word course.

This is a brief overview of Microsoft Word. With practice, you will become more proficient in using the software and its advanced features.

CHAPTER III

Overview of MS-Excel

Microsoft Excel is a popular spreadsheet software used for data analysis, organization, and management. Here is a complete guide to using Microsoft Excel:

1. Getting Started with Microsoft Excel:

- Launch Microsoft Excel on your computer.
- You will be greeted with the Start Screen, which offers various options to create a new workbook or open an existing one.
- Select the option that suits your needs.

1. Creating a New Workbook:

- To create a new workbook, select the "Blank workbook" option from the Start Screen or click on "New" from the File menu.
- Once you have created a new workbook, you can begin entering your data.

3. Entering Data:

- To enter data, click on a cell and start typing.
- You can use the arrow keys to navigate between cells, or you can use the mouse to click on the desired cell.
- You can also copy and paste data from other sources into Excel.

4. Formatting Data:

- To format data, select the cells you want to format and use the various options in the Home tab to change the font, size, color, and other formatting attributes.

- You can also use the Format Cells option to customize the formatting of your data.

5. Using Formulas and Functions:

- Excel provides various formulas and functions that can be used to perform complex calculations on your data.
- To use a formula or function, enter the formula or function in a cell, and Excel will calculate the result automatically.

6. Sorting and Filtering Data:

- Excel allows you to sort and filter your data based on various criteria.
- To sort data, select the data range you want to sort and click on the Sort button in the Data tab.
- To filter data, select the data range you want to filter and click on the Filter button in the Data tab.

7. Creating Charts:

- Excel allows you to create various charts to visualize your data.
- To create a chart, select the data range you want to use for the chart and click on the Charts button in the Insert tab.

8. Advanced Features:

- Microsoft Excel has many advanced features, such as PivotTables, conditional formatting, macros, and more.
- You can explore these features by using the Help menu or by taking a Microsoft Excel course.

9. Saving and Sharing:

- To save your workbook, click on the File menu and select "Save" or "Save As".
- You can also share your workbook with others by using the "Share" option in the File menu.

10. Printing:

- To print your workbook, click on the File menu and select "Print".
- You can also use the Print Preview option to preview your workbook before printing.

This is a brief overview of Microsoft Excel. With practice, you will become more proficient in using the software and its advanced features.

CHAPTER IV

Overview of MS-Power-point

Microsoft PowerPoint is a popular presentation software used to create slideshows for business presentations, lectures, and more. Here is a complete guide to using Microsoft PowerPoint:

1. Getting Started with Microsoft PowerPoint:

- Launch Microsoft PowerPoint on your computer.
- You will be greeted with the Start Screen, which offers various options to create a new presentation or open an existing one.
- Select the option that suits your needs.

1. Creating a New Presentation:

- To create a new presentation, select the "Blank presentation" option from the Start Screen or click on "New" from the File menu.
- Once you have created a new presentation, you can begin adding your content.

3. Adding Slides:

- To add a new slide, click on the New Slide button in the Home tab or right-click on the Slides pane and select "New Slide".
- You can choose from various slide layouts, including Title Slide, Title and Content, Two Content, Comparison, and more.

4. Adding Content:

- To add content to a slide, click on a placeholder and start typing.

- You can also insert various objects into your presentation, such as pictures, videos, tables, charts, and shapes.
- To insert an object, select the Insert tab and choose the appropriate option.

5. Formatting Slides:

- To format slides, select the slide you want to format and use the various options in the Home tab to change the font, size, color, and other slide attributes.

- You can also use the Themes and Variants options to quickly apply pre-defined styles to your presentation.

6. Using Transitions and Animations:

- PowerPoint allows you to add transitions between slides and animations to your objects.
- To add a transition, select the slide and click on the Transitions tab.
- To add an animation, select the object and click on the Animations tab.

7. Adding Speaker Notes:

- Speaker Notes allow you to add notes to your presentation that only you can see.
- To add speaker notes, click on the Notes button at the bottom of the screen.

8. Saving and Sharing:

- To save your presentation, click on the File menu and select "Save" or "Save As".

- You can also share your presentation with others by using the "Share" option in the File menu.

9. Presenting:

- To present your slideshow, click on the Slide Show tab and select "From Beginning".
- You can also use the Presenter View option to see your speaker notes and the next slide while presenting.

10. Printing:

- To print your presentation, click on the File menu and select "Print".
- You can also use the Print Preview option to preview your presentation before printing.

This is a brief overview of Microsoft PowerPoint. With practice, you will become more proficient in using the software and its advanced features.

CHAPTER V

Important shortcut keys

Here are some important shortcut keys for Windows computers:

1. General Shortcuts:

- Ctrl + C: Copy
- Ctrl + X: Cut
- Ctrl + V: Paste
- Ctrl + A: Select all
- Ctrl + Z: Undo
- Ctrl + Y: Redo
- Ctrl + F: Find
- Ctrl + S: Save
- Ctrl + P: Print
- Ctrl + Alt + Del: Open Task Manager
- Windows key + E: Open File Explorer

Here are some important shortcut keys for Windows computers:

1. General Shortcuts:

- Ctrl + C: Copy
- Ctrl + X: Cut
- Ctrl + V: Paste
- Ctrl + A: Select all
- Ctrl + Z: Undo
- Ctrl + Y: Redo
- Ctrl + F: Find
- Ctrl + S: Save
- Ctrl + P: Print
- Ctrl + Alt + Del: Open Task Manager

- Windows key + E: Open File Explorer

1. Windows Shortcuts:

- Windows key: Open Start menu
- Windows key + L: Lock computer
- Windows key + D: Show desktop
- Windows key + R: Open Run dialog box
- Windows key + I: Open Settings
- Windows key + Tab: Switch between open apps

3. Browser Shortcuts:

- Ctrl + T: Open a new tab
- Ctrl + W: Close current tab
- Ctrl + Shift + T: Reopen the last closed tab
- Ctrl + Shift + Delete: Clear browsing history
- Ctrl + F5: Refresh the current page

4. Microsoft Office Shortcuts:

- Ctrl + B: Bold text
- Ctrl + I: Italicize text
- Ctrl + U: Underline text
- Ctrl + S: Save
- Ctrl + N: Create a new document
- Ctrl + O: Open a document
- Ctrl + P: Print
- Ctrl + F: Find and replace
- F7: Spell check

These are just a few examples of the many shortcut keys available in Windows and various software applications. Learning and using these shortcuts can save you time and make you more efficient when using your computer.

CHAPTER VI

Necessity of Computers

The use of computers has become ubiquitous in today's society. Computers have revolutionized the way we work, play, and live. They offer a multitude of benefits, from increased productivity and efficiency to improved communication and collaboration. Computers also provide access to vast amounts of information, allowing users to quickly find what they need without spending hours hunting for it. Additionally, computers offer a variety of entertainment options, from streaming music to playing games. Furthermore, computers are increasingly being used in educational settings to help students prepare for real-world situations. With their powerful processing capabilities, computers can be used to simulate complex scenarios, giving students a better understanding of their subject matter. The benefits of computer usage are far-reaching and ever-expanding.

The use of computers has revolutionized the way we work, communicate, and live our lives. Computers offer a range of benefits, from increased productivity and enhanced communication to improved data management and efficient task automation. With the help of computers, businesses can easily store, access, analyze, and share data in real time. Additionally, businesses can use computers to automate repetitive tasks which helps reduce labor costs and increase efficiency. Computers also facilitate communication across businesses and organizations by enabling online meetings, video conferencing, and other forms of electronic communication. Furthermore, computers provide entertainment and education opportunities through the internet and various types of software. Finally, the use of computers has greatly enhanced the way people interact by connecting them with friends, family, and colleagues from around the world.

CHAPTER VII

Necessity of Internet

The Internet is a powerful medium that has had a profound effect on our lives. It has allowed us to connect with people from all over the world, access a wealth of information and create an online presence. It has enabled us to shop online, connect with our social networks, and even do our jobs remotely. The Internet has become an essential part of modern life, and it continues to evolve and develop with new technologies. It is estimated that over 4 billion people across the world have access to the Internet, making it one of the most influential communication tools in history. With the increasing availability of high-speed Internet access and mobile devices, the reach of the Internet is ever-expanding. It has revolutionized how we communicate, how we shop, and how we work. The Internet is transforming the way we live our lives and will continue to do so for generations to come.

The Internet is an invaluable tool that has revolutionized the world we live in by offering unprecedented access to information and communication. It has allowed people all around the world to connect with each other, exchange ideas, and work together on projects. It's also opened up new possibilities for businesses, allowing them to reach customers in new, innovative ways. The Internet has also opened up a new realm of entertainment options, such as streaming services, online gaming, and social media sites that have become incredibly popular. However, it is important to keep in mind that the Internet can be a double-edged sword. Unregulated websites can be a source of dangerous and inappropriate content, and data breaches can put important personal information at risk. As such, it is essential to use the internet responsibly, stay informed about security issues, and be aware of the risks associated with online activity.

CHAPTER VIII

Imortant points to remember

1. What is a computer?

A computer is essentially a machine that helps you do basic tasks such as accessing the internet, writing documents, and conducting basic calculations. You use a computer to make your everyday life easier.

A computer has many parts, including a monitor, keyboard, and mouse. You use these parts to interact with the computer. A monitor is where you see the computer's screen. You use the keyboard to type in commands and the mouse to move the cursor around the screen.

2. Components of a computer

Computers come in many different shapes and sizes, but all of them have certain basic components. In this section, we'll take a look at the most common components of a computer and how they work.

The motherboard is the brain of the computer. It contains all of the components that work together to turn your computer on and manage its functions. The motherboard is usually located on the bottom of the computer case.

The processor is the heart of the computer. It's part of the system that handles the most complex tasks. Processors come at different speeds and can be found in both desktop and laptop computers.

The RAM (random-access memory) is a type of memory that allows your computer to run multiple applications at the same time. RAM is also used to store temporary data, such as the results of a search.

The hard drive stores your programs, files, and photos. The hard drive is usually located in the computer's bottom-left corner.

The graphics card is responsible for rendering graphics on the screen. Most laptops and some desktops include a graphics card, while some computers have separate graphics cards for graphics-intensive tasks (like gaming) and for tasks that don't require high graphics (like browsing the Web).

The keyboard and mouse are the most common input devices. They allow you to interact with your computer in ways that are beyond simply typing in commands.

3. How a computer works?

A computer is made up of many different parts and each one of them is responsible for a specific task. In this article, we'll be discussing the different parts of a computer and how they work together to allow you to access the internet, write documents, play games, and more.

A computer starts off with a power supply that converts the electrical current into the correct format for the CPU, main memory, and graphics card. The CPU is responsible for running the operating system, applications, and drivers. The main memory is where data is temporarily stored while the graphics card handles all the graphics and animation.

The last part of the computer is the hard drive which stores all the files and programs you've used. You can access these files by opening the Start menu, typing "file explorer," and select the drive you want to open.

4. How to use a computer?

The guide will teach you how to use a computer. This includes how to open programs, navigate around the computer, use the internet, and more.

Computer basics are very important for anyone who wants to use the internet or do any sort of work on a computer. In this guide, we will cover the following topics:

- Opening programs
- Navigating around the computer
- Using the internet
- More

5. Internet and computer security

Make sure you take the necessary precautions to keep your computer and yourself safe online.

Computer security is a big topic and can be a little overwhelming. But don't worry, we're here to help. In this guide, we'll discuss the basics of computer security and how to protect yourself from the many dangers that the internet can hold.

We'll start by discussing the different types of threats and how to protect yourself from them. We'll also talk about the different ways to keep your computer safe online, including using a firewall, using a virus protection program, and using a password manager.

We'll also discuss the importance of computer security and how to protect yourself from identity theft and other forms of cybercrime. We'll finish the guide by providing some resources to further explore the topic.

6. How to start using a computer?

There is no need to be a computer expert to start using a computer. In fact, the majority of people don't even need to know how to use a mouse and keyboard. In this comprehensive guide, we'll teach you the basics of computer usage, from how to start your computer up, to using programs and files, to surfing the web, and more.

We'll start by explaining how to start your computer. After that, we'll take a look at using programs and files. We'll then move on to surfing the web and learning how to access different parts of the internet. We'll conclude the guide by giving you some tips on keeping your computer clean and safe.

So whether you're a beginner or an experienced computer user, this guide is perfect for you. Enjoy!

7. How to troubleshoot a computer?

If you're like most people, you use your computer for work, email, browsing the web, and maybe a little light gaming now and then. But did you know that even a little bit of misconfiguration or trouble can quickly turn into a full-blown computer disaster?

In this guide, we'll go over the basics of computer troubleshooting so you can get your machine back up and running as quickly as possible.

If your computer won't turn on, the first thing you should do is check to see if you've got power. If you don't have power, your computer is most likely not getting enough juice to start up. Next, make sure you've got enough storage space on your computer. If you're having trouble with your computer and you're not sure why it's a good idea to check to see if you're running out of storage space.

If your computer is functional but you're having problems with certain programs or files, your first step should be to try to re-install those programs or files. If that doesn't work, you may need to go ahead and reinstall your entire operating system.

If you're still having problems after trying all of the above, it's time to call in the experts. A qualified computer technician can diagnose and fix most problems with your computer in a matter of minutes.

8. Troubleshooting software

When you're having trouble with your computer, the last thing you want to do is try to fix it yourself. Even if you think you know what you're doing, chances are you don't. And if you do end up

fixing it yourself, you might make things worse.
Here are some tips for troubleshooting software.

If you're having problems with an application, try reinstalling it.

If you're having problems with your computer's hardware, try resetting it.

If you're having problems with your internet connection, try checking your router and cables.

If you're having problems with your computer's operating system, try upgrading it. If you're having problems with a program, try uninstalling it and then reinstalling it.

9. How to stay safe online?

As technology advances, so too does the level of cybercrime. In fact, according to a study from the FBI, cybercrime cost businesses a total of $445 billion in 2016. That's an increase of more than 6% from the year before and it's expected to reach $5 trillion by 2021. That's why it's so important to be proactive when it comes to online safety. Here are a few tips to help you stay safe.

1. Use a strong password:
Make sure your password is at least 8 characters long and contains at least one number and one letter.

2. Don't click on suspicious links:
Don't click on links contained in unsolicited emails, as these are often laden with malware.

3. Update your software:
Make sure you update your software and browser plugins as soon as

they become available.

4. Use a VPN:
A virtual private network (VPN) encrypts your traffic and prevents anyone from tracking your online activity.

5. Be cautious with social media:
Be cautious about what you post on social media and be sure to only share information that you would feel comfortable sharing with your friends.

6. Use antivirus software:
Make sure you install antivirus software on your computer and use it regularly to scan for malicious software.

7. Use two-factor authentication:
Two-factor authentication is a great way to add an extra layer of security to your accounts.

8. Keep track of your financial data:
Make sure you keep track of your bank and credit card account numbers, as well as your login information.

9. Educate yourself:
It's never too late to learn about online safety. There are plenty of resources available online, and even some great apps that make it easy to keep track of your online activity.

Conclusion

Computer basics are essential in any online business. In this guide, we've covered everything from PC hardware to internet browsers. Whether you're just starting out or you're looking to improve your current skills, you'll find everything you need in this guide.
We hope you've found this guide helpful and that it will help you get started on the right foot. Please feel free to leave a comment if you have any questions or suggestions.

We hope you enjoyed our book about computer basics. We know that there are a lot of things that you need to know in order to use a computer effectively, and we wanted to make sure that we covered everything in this post. We also have a helpful info graphic that you can use as a reference. We hope that this post has helped you feel more confident about using a computer and that you will continue to use it for years to come! Thank you for reading, and we hope to see you next time!

Printed by Libri Plureos GmbH in Hamburg,
Germany